Always Something Heartfelt

Always Something Heartfelt

Ashton Harper

ashton.harper@gmail.com

ISBN 979-8-218-20415-0

Printed in the United States of America

First Printing, 2024

For the girls

Contents

Part V

Notes from the Author

For all of those who helped me along the way—to the many who inspired the words; to all of you who have made this book a part of your collection—I say thank you!

This book is about the many phases of my life, which for a while was centered around love and its pursuit, usually ending up in dissatisfying disappointment.

I hope you enjoy.
I hope you can relate.
I pray you never have to see yourself in my negative fates.
I wish you all the happiness your heart can stand.
I wish you Always Something Heartfelt!

Always Something Heartfelt

Part I

He Say, She Say, They Say

Sometimes,
when observing a tree up close
it's hard to see the beauty that it entails.
Sometimes,
you need to take a step or two back.
They say it's hard to be in love.
I say love is what you make it.
They say you only get one,
maybe two true loves in your lifetime.
I say I have truly loved many,
and many have truly loved me.
I say I'm nothing like anything you ever experienced in a man
and they say, you too sure of yourself,
but at the same time
they say don't be afraid to shine baby.
I say didn't they say our biggest fear is not that we are inadequate?
I say yes, I am confident and I know where I'm going cause GOD guides my ship,
and you know what they say,
with GOD guiding you, you can't lose,
or at least that's what he says, my pastor.
He told me that He'll never leave me or forsake me, GOD.
And I know that to be true.

They say people come into your life for reasons, seasons, lifetimes, and treasons in some cases,
and that if you hold to a season, for whatever reason,
you'll miss out on your lifetime,
but how are we to be so sure?
She says I'm her reason for waking up and breathing.
I say that sounds like a lifetime.
But we're not together anymore so,

how are we to be so sure?
She says, I can't help it or that's just the way women are and that's what they do.
I say that's bullshit because every day we choose,
we choose to love, laugh, and cry—correction,
we choose to deal with that emotion that comes with a laugh or a cry
cause I say and I've always said, your emotions are the truest things about you,
and you choose to take offense when a stranger doesn't acknowledge you
and it's only the two of you in the room.
You choose to be mad when someone steps on your shoe in the club.
You choose to get involved in all that humbug!
All that he said, she said, nonsense
or maybe you don't choose,
because they say we are a product of our experiences.
So maybe your reaction at 25 was fueled by what you saw at 10 and thought was ok.
You know what I always say, you are who you are by the time you are about hmm about 17.
So that 40-year-old man that's playing games with you ladies, he wasn't taught any better.
His life experiences didn't take him down that relationship path;
it was just him and Mom, til he was about 23.
She says she was trying to shield him from that,
the nonsense Mom was going through with all the unfit men she encountered,
including the one she fondled and made you with.
She said she was trying to protect her son from him,
the one who injected the seed,
his supposed rightful male role model.
He said he couldn't deal with it or wasn't ready to be a man,
he was just trying to get some and get back to playing his video games
because he said

he never got to do it as a child.
Besides, video games help with my motor skills.
I'm trying to get my hand-eye coordination up,
he says and his boys confirm
he was just trying to get a nut
and she said she was on the pill
but she said she forgot to take it that day,
because she usually takes it with her meal
around 9 o'clock,
but that night
she didn't eat. . . .
I say it is what it is
you got a seed . . . now what?
They say if you aren't careful this life will take
you by your knees.
I say please!
It's never as bad as it seems when staring directly
at that tree. . . .
Take a step back,
trust in yourself, and believe!

Blessed Perspective

I'll be whatever you want me to be
It's very interesting, we sometimes believe
Things we never see
And never see things we believe
But we believe, like if I just wish on it long enough
It'll be
Or if I just stop pissing him off, he won't beat me, maybe
Maybe it's me
I have it backward, I believe in things that are in
Front of me and that have proven to be
Like GOD
And I know that may seem contradictory but I see
He, more than any
It's like my momma said: "That tree is growing and
It has nothing to do with me"
I can get up and be in my right mind to once again
Attempt to live this life circumspectly
And free. . . .
Free of all the ills I have created in my past; free
Of the guilt of behaving crass
Free to know that this too shall pass. . . .

The Plea

Before I cry and plead
Break another heart or destroy another soul
Before someone else turns cold toward me
So that I won't open another nose that can't be
Closed without a relationship with me
Please send me what I need

I'm Alone

I'm alone, but at least it's quiet
My soul is intact
I did the right thing so . . . no looking back
I'm alone, but my world hasn't stopped turning
New friends and destinations
But of course, there's a yearning, but I'm learning
I'm learning
I'm alone, and I've been here before, but
Never this intoxicating
I can't hold this one down like I used to
Because of maturity, I'm scratching
The useless fornicating
It's just fabricating a lie
Cause even when you're here I'm still alone. DAMN
That's enough to make you cry
I understand if, at this point, you want to say
Your goodbyes
I'm alone, but tis nothing new
I've been here before and right now my color is red
Not blue
Red cause it's bold–if it were blue, I'd still be cold
Or cool whatever the hue representation
Without hesitation I lean on my patience and in
That, I find time for a celebration
Yeah I'm alone, but at least there's no frustration,
No senseless confrontation, just confirmation
That this is where I need to be–GOD and me
Harmony, sweet harmony
So I'm alone, still with a small quaint itch to fish,
For something new
Slow down baby, I'm alone but not stupid
I didn't mean you
And I didn't mean to mislead you
And I know when I leave, you'll be lonely too

And I really do empathize with you baby, but sometimes
You gotta do, what cha gotta do
And I gotta do me
On some DMX prayer skit like
"There was something that, I just had to see, that
You wanted me to see, so I could be what you
Wanted me to be. . .."
But unlike X, I haven't seen yet
I'm alone, trying not to let this dig into my chest
All while I'm trying not to pay attention to her breasts
And I'm gonna try not to suggest that we lay down
That she come hang out in my town
Because it would be a waste
Waste of time, waste of energy, and a disgrace
Cause you'll have a good time, I'm sure
In the bed, on the floor, holding on to the door
Etc, etc. . . . yeah that's my name
And now I'm up on your sexual wall of fame
Game Set Match
You're hooked, I'm not
Just an itch I needed to scratch, in fact not even a need
And what we're really doing right now
Is setting ourselves up for an unwanted seed
Yeah, I'm alone; I know you heard it before, sure
But understand I'm not complaining
GOD has it all under control
So I'm alone, but I'm patiently waiting

You Are Not Grown

You are not grown. . . .
It is far too great for you to understand or grasp,
But it's simple.
You tend to believe you are managing but you're
Missing it, and thus missing out on life.
I'd preach to you forgiveness and how it would save
Your life but you have to understand your strife.
But you are afraid.
Maybe you are ashamed with nothing to be
Embarrassed about.
Can you stand naked in the mirror, or can you
Stomach being alone with your thoughts?
At this point it's not others who are harming you; there
Isn't blame to be placed anywhere else; squarely
I pity you and your pretentious declarations of change.
Sometimes drifters go out too far.
Swimming requires control and conquer of the waves.
You, my dear, are being tossed in violent turbulence.
Waves so chaotic they're keeping you afloat,
Tossing you back and forth so much
You are standing still.
But you are drowning,
shipwrecked without a clue,
out in a place where only GOD can save you.
So I'll continue to pray.

You Are Out of Position Get Up

You are in the wrong position; ACTUALLY, you're out of
position.
You say you're waiting on the revolution.
Well, you're out of position.
I have sat and listened to the petitions,
descriptions, and consequences of our actions.
I can almost recite them forwards and backward and
still here we are—
steadily declining, all of us are dying.
Those whose lives were captured by violence, low
tolerance, and despair,
they're ahead of the game, just cashing
in on what was saved.
The Bible says "A man born of a woman
shall surely die. . . ."
And still, we rave, "Stop the Violence, Increase the
Peace! Stop the Killing, Save our Street!
Decrease the beef, increase the beat,"
or something to that effect.
Rallies for everyone to check in or speak their
peace, and speak we do.
I have sat and listened to the petitions,
descriptions, and consequences of our actions.
We say it's the government's fault, the parents.
We gather stats and data—
numbers mean nothing more than the dream of a
peaceful reality, unfathomable,
as worthless as the paper we print them on—ashes,
statisticians can't keep up. . . .
We could use SportsCenter's stat room to tally up the
number of murders, robberies, and senseless acts of
violence,
but they can't measure the hatred, racism, and
prejudice inside us, all of us.

The people in this room walked past each
other and didn't speak.
This leads me to believe without a doubt that you're
out of position for the revolution you seek.
It tells me you don't even know where
the hell you need to be.
But I'm sure you were in the conversation at that
rally last week about peace
can't even spell the phrase "making a difference."
All we do is talk and I'm tired of listening.
I have sat and listened to the petitions,
descriptions, and consequences of our actions,
but I stopped paying attention; I was busy.
Busy keeping my siblings and cousins out of Saturday
detentions, or suspensions.
In short, I was mentoring
and you got the start in your household, so I don't
encourage them to fight or try to act grown.
I encourage them to excel, stay far away from jail,
and be sure to pray.
Hell is not your home, it's just where we dwell.
And what the hell were you doing last Saturday or on
a weekly afternoon?
Do you check on the kids in your family? Have you
ever visited a neighborhood school? Participated in
a career day?
We supposed to be on the same team.
Are you not also tired of the senseless violence?
Isn't that why you showed up to complain when the
mayor cut the budget for police officers?
Didn't it piss you off when they cut the education
budget and closed all the local schools?
Not trying to be rude but, you're a fool if you think
the solution to our problems is in last week's rally
or this morning's radio conversation.
Or the bill passed updating whatever beneficial
financial allocations.
I have sat and listened to the petitions,
descriptions, and consequences of our actions.

As far as I'm concerned, that's part of the problem—
you think because you talked about it and got your
idea on the table,
somehow our economy will magically become more stable.
That we'll be able to save the upcoming generation,
who by the way are never at the table
for these conversations.
This equation doesn't require rocket science,
if you want to stop the violence, get up out of your
chair; I told you, you were out of position. . . .
Develop a bond with those around you, let 'em know
you'll be there.
And we are all in this together.
Volunteer a few hours and cut back on some of that
time you spend on doing or cutting your hair,
or the time you spend lounging in your favorite
chair, with your favorite boy or girl.
Give random people some love;
say hi, be polite and kind.
Perform random acts of kindness when no one is around.
Bring to any and every situation positive energy—
Fourth Chapter, Eight Verse of Philippians.
I have sat and listened to the petitions,
descriptions, and consequences of our actions
and I agree that's where we had to start but we're
300 years past that point.
Now it's time to get up and do something, more than
just your part; that's not all you can do—
focus all your energy on any and everything
positive, right, good, and true.
That revolution you're looking for, starts with you.
Get ya ass up!

What Kind

What kind of person lies on a good man?
What kind of people praise you and work to take everything you had?
What kind of friend doesn't give you a call
to ask you if you're ok or what's going on?
What kind of person talks to you for four hours and doesn't say a word?
What kind of a woman tells you you're amazing
but doesn't believe in you at all?
How easy was it for you to be convinced I was wrong?
What kind of mother always takes everyone else's side?
What kind of mother decides the right thing to do to her son is call the cops?
What kind of mother pretends to console you for something she's done?
She orchestrated the shit and was like
"I know, I know son."
What kind of man participates in something so foul?
What kind of elder dismisses you when you cry out?
What kind of woman pledges until the end of time and then abandons you in broad daylight?
What kind of people seek to take everything you love?
When even what they are taking has nothing to do
with what they perceived was wrong. . . .
What kind of people you've often given your last,
literally turn their back on you like you don't matter?
What kind of family sits and watches you like you're a pedophile while you try to spend time with your child?
What kind of woman you are, helping to contribute to a bullshit plot?
What kind of man takes care of another man's child
just like it's his own? Only to find out the mother doesn't believe in you at all.
What kind of brother doesn't truly believe in your dreams?

What kind of brother doesn't give you the game to
help you succeed?
What kind of brother doesn't help you out
when you are down?
The same brother who has helped you all of your life?
What kind of people let you suffer knowing they can
help you out?
What kind of person distances themselves from those
who hurt him?
What kind of man moves on with his life?
All kinds of people exist in this world
and mistakes get made.
Everyone will hurt you no matter what they've said. . . .
There will come a time when you are truly alone in life—
you have got to determine for yourself that you are
important enough to stay alive.
You will have to forgive all trespassers,
no matter what kind.

Life in the Big City

she was looking for the man that she could
let go and confess
that her love was his and she didn't want it back
there he was sitting nicely dressed, full of
kindness, compassion, and intelligence to match
there the two sat but she never noticed him, because
he was too nice
guess that's life
life in the big city

he's chosen a few at times from all parts of the country
some good pretenders but all leave him lonely
hope it's the right one at the right time, becoming
weary of it all and apprehensive to try
tired of the tireless arguments and unwarranted strife
thinking to himself: "this can't be life. . . ."
life in the big city

a young man pours out his heart to capture
a woman's soul
and she, offering him nothing in return
as her ex took it all and is now gone, sadly, she
doesn't know he cannot take that which is hers
but she prefers ignorance mistaken for scorn, keeping
her past comfortably in sight
never opening up to see if this man could be right
is this real life
life in the big city

he sits and waits on his unaware deadbeat dad
with her not having the courage to tell him, he is
never coming back
pretty sad, but that is life
life in the big city

he sits on a gold mine unbeknownst to him, his way with words irony, and sarcasm
the intelligent mind never looking inside, concerned with outward appearance, perceptions, and lies
to prove his worth, he slings some pies, but the dope game was never for him
they shot and killed him in cold blood, 38 times
and they call that life
life in the big city

I call it pity
a pity we sometimes can't, don't, won't, or refuse to see past our right nows
not realizing, remembering, or believing there is a GOD that hears our cries
and just past the horizon, right on the other side
there is far more to this life
this life in the big city

and there is more to life than self-pity
more than living just enough for the city

Sexual Experiences

How exactly do you measure the value
of a sexual experience?
Now, before you make your attempt to answer this question
this isn't about the physical erection manifesting
inside her walls.
This isn't about that night of passion
that transcended time,
or that sweet moment you share after the candles and wine.
Consider this,
two lust-struck strangers, trapped in time, or
engulfed in the present
intrigued by physical attributes
concentrating solely on their temporary connection. . . .
They are obviously . . .
having a great time . . .
and decide to go back to her place to unwind.
At that time, things get heated, and a night of
passion ensues.
A night that becomes the beginning of a new chapter
in the lives of the two. . . .
A month later, the lady finds out she's pregnant,
pregnant for a man she knew all of less than 24
hours at the time of conception.
How is this sexual experience measured?
We call this—the mistake.
But it's never a mistake to be a part of GOD's
creation and conception in time.
We'll just call the measure of this sexual experience
LIFE.

Life; their life—
married and cheered, shared and nurtured, love
cultivated for years.
Years of soft kisses, passionate intermissions, no

remission, just an honest love petition.
They are the epitome of love; love is now the definition–
they no longer have sex.
In fact, when they make love
the earth tends to fall from its orbit, the rivers
stop flowing, words no longer take form,
and even GOD stops and takes a moment's notice like,
"Yeah, that's it; that's how it was intended."
This sexual experience is defined as transcending!
Better than your first kiss, better than the cool
breeze on a heated day;
as good as your favorite ice cream served your
favorite way;
more potent than your most precious moment.
On second thought, the measure of this sexual
experience has got to be eternal.
As in long-lasting, a forever moment,
indefinable by chapters.
Unable to be trapped under the ink stains of a book;
inevitable like death or unstoppable like Jordan's
dominance and Kareem's hook.
But I digress. . . .
A trickster–better known as a master of deception–
she's kept you at bay for years, your sexual
equal it appears,
and it appears to be what we often define as fidelity.
The only man with whom she's ever been connected;
she was a virgin.
Her essence belongs to you
forever etched in history as her first time and her
first love. . . .
At all times she seems sweet as a dove–you loved,
she loved harder.
You gave; she gave.
But this gift wasn't a kind one;
deception and lies embodied
as the doctor tells you, you are the father of a
sexual disease. Somebody has been lying. . . .
Now you sit–

sad, confused, heated, and furious far past any
point of reasoning!
But the feeling that defines this experience is
heartbreak, it ain't even about the diseases.
See, you never imagined or dreamed a day like this
would ensue.
When you woke up this morning you prayed, shortly
thereafter you bathed, made sure you touched up your
fade, and headed out to the doctor for your routine
checkup–
who knew that now your doctor visit would have to
become regular?
But all you can think about is how your dreams have
been shattered and scattered into microscopic pieces,
like a grain of sand being split and divided into
six million pieces.
What's the peace or contentment in this situation?
How do you measure a sexual experience of this nature?
This event is bigger than you and her having sex.
It's more about her having sex with him, before he
has sex with her, after which, she had sex with that
boy, and that boy was with that one, that one, and
that one–
a line so long, you don't know
what the fuck is going on.
At this point, all you know for sure is that you have
been cheated on.
And now . . .
you have this constant reminder, that outlasts any
physical scar–pain.
Like slamming the hammer down and finding the nail
has been replaced by your finger.
Like the hammer being COCKED, pulled, one let loose
from the chamber.
Like dying and finding out you were in fact a lost soul,
destined to make hell your home. . . .
It's cold.
Tragedy is the word that comes to mind, like the
moor from Shakespearean times.

Something you can't prepare for, so you'll never be ready.
This sexual experience is a tragedy of deception,
but we'll just call the measure of this sexual experience
heavy.
Like the 2005 breach of the levees,
like leaving your daughter in a room to get molested
and you get her tested
and she has HIV.
Geezzz!
Always be careful–
how do your sexual experiences get measured?

Why

why is it that the people closest to you who
supposedly think the highest of you,
make the worst assumptions about you?
is it because they also know the worst of you?
don't the people closest to you deserve the biggest
benefit of the doubt?
or do they feel like it's ok to make those
assumptions about you,
because they assume you know the best of them
and so you know they didn't mean it?
backwards, maybe.
why are we so hard on ourselves, but when others make
comments we go
"that's just the way I am."
I mean, don't get me wrong,
it's not right to pass judgment but what if it's
constructive?
why are we never satisfied?
we search for something, get it, and figure out ways
to cause it to die.
why rock the boat when it's fine?
or invent new crimes or reasons to be mad?
why not let bygones be bygones and enjoy the moment?
why question good quality time?
leave y by the z and hold on to the e and enjoy the ride.

Jumping

What good is this if we can't dance naked in the rain?
What good is this if this doesn't drive us insane?
What good is this if I am scared to jump?
And what good is this if I'm not willing to dive in
front of the truck?
Stand in front of that firing squad?
Wait—
I am.
But it's your turn now.
I keep checking to see what you'll do.
I should be a man and jump without waiting on you.
You'll be there if that's really what you want.
As for me,
I just need to trust in He—
that even if you're not there to catch me,
He will always be.

Part II

Plutonic

I hesitated to tell this tale or any tale of the sort.
It's not that I am incapable; it's just . . .
I try not to deal in storybooks.
So in turn, I've determined to give her something of worth.
Surely, she'd want that, I hoped.
So this story doesn't go once upon a time in a
faraway land.
It doesn't begin in my head and it has nothing to do
with the last stand.
Or someone's hand in marriage.
There is no what had happened was. . . .
It's not about anything that was or ever will be.
But it's a true story.
Sometime in the short past, a man stumbles upon a woman,
for so brief an instance.
Probably could be considered an accident.
For in a moment, life led them in different directions–
he, new beginnings elsewhere,
and she encountered her transgressions–
battles of the sickened, continuously bedridden.
All after their meeting at the tail end of winter.
Spring–
the season of new growth, constant showers, and change,
but for both, it continually rained,
pushing them further from their newly acquainted days.
A two-time event
presented as a friendship after such
a microscopic instance.
Instantaneously a success.
And however short-lived both proved their friendship
wasn't worth putting to rest.
Or as is the assessment of the man,
not sure what was in the woman's hand.
I'm sure it was innocence but who knows.

And the man wasn't overzealous or eager to know.
Guess it would just make for a completed state. . . .
Poker face–
I believe the man wanted to change the stakes.
But steadfast, jaded, and disciplined, she managed to stay in her lane;
she has her reasons.
For I'm sure as they approach new seasons, she thinks about the days becoming cold.
And no matter how much you try
visits from the distance are never enough to hold over in the trenches of winter.
No matter how much you try,
you can't make absence a catalyst where
a body mass should do.
And no matter how much you try
there is nothing like a random Tuesday pass-through.
Or an often taken-for-granted "I'll meet you there."
There is nothing like "Are we having dinner
here or over there?"
And the man,
he understands, or so she hopes.
In her head, she seems to believe she's been here before–
implications that she does this all the time.
And he's sure she has . . . doesn't matter to the man–
same script different cast.
Where they are now though–they seem to be having a blast.
Walking a tightrope and laughing about the past,
giving each other fits about the future.
He's like "I think we should . . ." and she's like
"Not interested, Boo."
"Or look me up when you get in town, but not just with your samsonite."
Consistent conversation over the span of one night,
enlightening perspectives taking things to new heights.
This is the story of two individuals
seemingly out innocently dancing with no fancy of flight.
A One-way ticket to nowhere in particular–
nonstop.

Tamed

I have all these mushy feelings
I thought it best not to contact you with them
Wasted energy
No synergy
It's weird that you are present yet inaccessible
I can reach but I can't have you
That's hard
Our energy is strong
Long and longstanding
Hard to manage and maintain
Hard to imagine it contained
Still, I refrain
Far too much pain
Nothing left to gain
It's an interesting concept to be tamed

Under Appreciation

he spends a lifetime or his span on Earth putting
himself in a position to be what she wants him to be.
she says she prefers ambition, he tries to conquer
the world.
she then says he doesn't spend enough time at home.
she wants six children they have all boys.
she says, "why didn't you give me any girls?"
he cries in her arms, tells her all of his fears, and
lets go of all his bad dreams.
they argue, and she says, "I think you're weak."
what do you want from me?
I exercise patience and restraint
then I don't care or I'm too nice.
I get upset.
I have a temper problem.
I plead my case.
I'm combative and intolerable.
I get jealous.
I'm being insecure.
I chase you–
you say I'm overzealous.
I leave you–
then I can't get it, because I wasn't persistent–
are you kidding?
what the hell I am supposed to do?
what do you want from me?

Restraint

Expressions seem to fall on deaf ears
I don't usually carry tears unless you count sadness
I got a bag of that shit with your name on it
As if
Words typically escape you
But interestingly enough actions do too
We've talked through your lack of words of expression
The action is lacking
Your proclamations demand more than presence
For how you say feel
You'd be the one helluva triathlete
Gold medals galore
A performance unparalleled
Instead there is a fog so thick it's paralyzing
Suffocating and confining
Your candle is out but not raised high
Decommissioned lighthouse
No longer standing waiting at the shore
A show from behind a proverbial curtain
An undercover cop pretending but lurking
Lots of potential energy
Not worth it I guess
Wasted expression
Not worthy I guess

Consolation Prize

Though not perfect by a long shot you show
Signs of seeing me
Some of the gestures more impactful than I think you
Could even see
Without an attitude you'd be perfection
Despite that reaction to past afflictions you still
Gather my acceptance
You're kind
You amaze
I will always cherish those days
I'll take being partially seen over being flat-out
Ignored always

I Fell

I feel defeated beaten and worn down
The 9th hour of my 9th life in the bottom of the inning
With the bottom of the order coming up
Down by one
The 1.67 batting avg Pitcher
No swagger having ass henchmen
That guy is pinch-hitting
Cancer out of remission
Season finale bullshit happily ever after shit
You know the kind of storyline where you're upset
Like "That's how this ended"
"Really"
Really that's how I'm feeling
Winded
As you know you're too old to be playing
Confused
Like Japanese being whispered
Nothing I can understand
I am suffering
My stomach rumbling but everything coming up
Dead rodent stench
Immensely in pain
Favorite shirt stain
Bad guy constantly showing up where the hero would save
No fairy tales, Anita
What have I done, Neo
I am not the one
The least favorite of the worst ones
The fall was gradual
Then rapid
Death on white waters
Pain

You Don't Want Me

You don't want me and I'm starting to wonder if you
ever really did.
As kids in college, I yearned for you.
At age 25 I still want you,
as I always did.
Fear, apprehension, or disbelief—
all I have seemed to be floating in the air.
An aroma of doubt always sprouts.
What haven't I said, or what is it that I did or
didn't do?
Six years and still no me and you.
To me, they all get compared,
all unprepared or they don't measure up.
I'm him—you know it, so do I.
So why the front?
Or is it reality looking me in the face?
If you don't want me, then I can't take my rightful place
as your man, lover, husband, and friend.
Same ole tired excuses over and over and over again
guarded by past pain.
It's cool with brand-new Cats
but this ain't the same type of game.
I'm in a league of my own—
sorry about the arrogance and hostile tone.
But it's clear the frustration clouds my better judgment.
Acceptance is what's missing.
Neither of us has been perfect—
save the talk about I did you wrong
and fuck what that other kid did—he's gone,
left under his own power.
Hour after hour I sit and ponder—
what have I done or didn't do;
why is it that no matter what happens
YOU STILL don't seem to want me?
But I've ALWAYS WANTED YOU.

Depression

My head is cloudy
I can feel it
I've been feeding my brain chocolates
For months
Maybe even years
Not even clear enough to cry tears
Abandoned and judged by my peers
Because of the little ears
I guess I was reckless enough one too many times
Like I haven't washed away their grime
Did it for years
I'm living in fear
Get queasy every time I think of moving
What am I supposed to say
When she asked "What brings you here today"
My mind is cloudy and my world is grey
I'm full of inaction
I lack passion
And courage
I really don't know what to do
I'm confused scared and lonely
I feel like a total fool
I literally don't know what to do

Temporary Insanity

She posed the question:
"Ashton, are you ready for a relationship?"
I smiled for a minute and asked, "Are you asking me to be in one?"
Her rebuttal: "Can you just answer the question?"
As if I was her son.
I tickled her fancy–
"At this point in my life, giving the pending arrival, I have to wait and see."
I figured this would alter her answer to my question;
I did just give her a maybe.
And then there was silence, and she spoke not a word.
Music filled the void with a soft undertone–
"Cause everybody knows . . ."
A tragedy I've called it, one of fear and passiveness and she'd think I was stabbing at her or taking shots but I'm not.
Because my fear of her never coming back to me caused me to never stop.
I never stop going back to the tree to see which she wanted to be with me.
Some had temporary lasting power,
most were for the night.
Ms. Right? Hi I'm Mr. Right Now–
just Manish.
And now I've managed to change the entire course of my life.
So now her mood has changed and I'm confused.
I've been singing the same song for years!
And now . . .
now it's like "Alright homie this is it . . ."
but coach I've been sitting at the end of this bench COLD.
I still got my sweats on and now you hit me with the

"Let's bring this one home"
on some "Win one for the Gipper."
So now you wanna try on my glass slipper?
Cool, it's over in my fairytale box!
Along with the engagement ring, magic carpet, trick spindle,
and the three blind mice.
There was a frog there too, but the poor thing suffocated and died.
I tried; I swear to GOD I did–
maybe my efforts weren't as big as I thought.
Here's a thought–
is this about loneliness?
Dude's gone for good and now I'm back in?
Is this because I was always waiting
or my feelings never changed?
Is this like one of those after-school
specials where they're like
"I was wrong, can we try again?"
Now out of the blue, I have your full undivided attention?
Is there something you're not mentioning? I mean really what's the deal?
Am I the flavor of the moment? This can't be real!
This sounds like a taste of temporary insanity!
Set to vanish.
Once another is SEEMINGLY Manish enough to chill or has that windy city appeal.

Jury Duty

I am the only Monster on the planet
Everyone else needs to be forgiven
I am to be destroyed and banished

One to Grow With

I go through your photos at least a dozen times a week
They often make me weak
In a good and bad way
I've run out of things to say
I feel stupid
You've taken your stance
Though I don't understand it is out of my league
I cannot compete with or argue about what
You feel you need
I believe our love is unique but I'm not naïve
There are a million different combinations of love
We both know it's by choice that you are alone
Every time I see your face I melt
I want to run to you
Every time we communicate
I want to
Still there's no relief
There's nothing I can say to make you want me
What if it's never this strong
What if you're wrong
It's hard to be wrong about who you are
Growing with this one is so hard

Remnants

I do miss you
But with you I have experienced both heaven and hell
And unfortunately
Heaven was but a dream
Fallacy
A mirage in the desert
I woke up to a newscast showing last
Week's lottery numbers
I had a ticket with those same numbers for this
Week's drawings
Imagine my disappointment
After careful consideration it was all hell
I believe you wanted to love me but didn't know how
You've gotten so used to faking it
I'm not your guy
I never was
I did however show you love
Smitten swimming drowning shit
Life-giving
Ready to give life trying to give you life
When we
Don't get me started on that part
Fake news
Listen I love you with all my heart and all the
Other parts of me
And I believe you wanted to love me back
Or at least that's what I want to believe
Now that I know I was sold one
I get to make up my own dreams

A Reader

I just want to be seen
Without being heard
Just once
In any aspect of my life
Someone to leave the instructions in the box
And just have me all figured out
I just want someone to care
Estimate me accurately with accuracy
Or just follow the guidebook
Either way works for me
As long as they know how to read

Alone Again

I'd forgotten what this was like
I am sipping from a bone-dry cup
In love with a 36-day-old corpse
Sitting with my arm around it
I'm at the starting line of a track at a
Katrina-ravaged park
Waiting on my turn to play hopscotch or double-Dutch
With the children of the Holocaust

I am alone

I feel stuck
Like those not married for love
Like most of society, in a job, they don't really want
But the bills have to get paid
I am parked in a sand dune of mud

Alone

I am canvassing the coast of Japan looking for
Surviving surfers
Having dinner with John Kennedy and his murderer
Looking for words of encouragement from this now
150-day-old dead woman
Sitting on a 400-passenger train with only its driver

I'm alone, but I'll be a lonely survivor

Part III

Dead Memories

I can look through your photos
I see all the details of your curvature
The fluctuation in weight
But I don't remember anything
What it was like to feel you in my hand
Your chest and nipples between my teeth
I don't remember any of it
What exactly am I holding on to
The pictures
The videos
You are one of the greatest tragedies
We had so much potential
So much damage
Still contending it was far less than those before
I am no judge
And I get it I really do
But what am I holding on to

I Got Lost

I got lost
Somewhere in between me and whom they wanted me to be
Whom they told me I should be
Whom they told me I shouldn't be or couldn't be
Or was
I got lost
There is this fog
Hazy
Always causes me to feel off
Every once and a while I get going
Then momentum falls wayside high
I got lost
I just want to go forward
Why does it seem like so many want to hold me back
Or have me in the place they think I should be
We won't promote you until you act like thee
You can't love like that or you can but not with me
I need you to be like thee
I got lost
Stagnant
Stale
I stopped trying and I don't know why
Yet I keep trying to get out
Cyclic
Looper
Won't be long before I'm before me
I want someone to support me
Wholeheartedly
They tell me I don't need it
They tell me to stop waiting on it
But they all have that backing
Did mine get lost
I really don't know how to get out
I am lost

People Don't Just Up and Leave

You're mistaken–
it's not that easy to walk away from someone you love.
If it seems easy or that it happens at a moment's notice to you,
that means you were not paying attention;
what actually happened is that the person was dealing with whatever problems longer than you realized.
The person had probably been crying out to you in some manner
in which you were not observant enough to recognize,
too arrogant to realize,
too selfish to care about,
or you just flat-out ignored it.
Whatever the case may be, you missed the boat.
And when you finally decided to look up, pay attention, or seek understanding, it was too late.
Nobody just gets up and walks away from something that they invest their time and energy into in any capacity.
Most of us have a hard time saying goodbye, letting go and/or accepting change in general,
so how is it that we could just walk away without any warning signs?
Is that really a realistic perspective?
Or is that your excuse for not paying attention
and not having enough wherewithal to realize things were changing right in front of you?
Now whether they changed because of your actions or outside forces,
you have to figure that out on your own.
One thing you must OWN is that people do not change overnight,
and for whatever reason, you missed the transition,
tried to deny it, or did nothing to prevent it.
Most times people don't just up and leave

so when it appears to be that,
it just means they were suffering longer than you were able to see.

Treacherous

I have made a ton of mistakes
Done some folks wrong
I can own my flaws
I must have been worse than I thought
I was apparently bad for business and friendship
Some things get lost
Worn down at times
I am no throwaway
Am I?
Judgment gets heavier outside the lines
The stories don't matter just the end results

This Is What We Do

Separation and heartache make us extremely flustered.
We start to consider and ponder all sorts of ideas,
most unhealthy ones.
We think, "Was it something I could have done better?"
"What if I never find another person like them?"
"What if I never find another person, period?"
"What am I gonna do?"
"I wonder if they miss me
or what they're doing and who they're doing it with,"
to the point that it drives us madly insane
cause we cannot openly stomach the idea of truly
living this life alone.
The emptiness is far too much to bear and we have
way too much time to think.
They did say an idle mind is the devil's workshop.

And then just that fast we met someone new,
someone to help ease the loneliness-
to make us feel special again;
to love us.
Secretly we hope they'll help us pick up the pieces.
Jaded by our last experience, our hunger
for that feeling,
that sweet soft inviting euphoric feeling-
our hunger increases.
And we cling to this situation tighter than the last
without even realizing it,
every intimate moment taking our breath away.

Just as the flame begins to fuel at its highest,
we want nothing than to be closer to it.
It allures you,
to detriment.
Because you either smother it or it consumes-

either way, the fire is gone
leaving us emptier than dry bones in a desert land.
Destitute,
only to begin the process again.

Patience

now and again
you have moments where it feels like
you're running in place
like no matter which direction you run in
you wind up back in the same spot
sort of stuck in rut
remember these possibilities
one can still burn calories on a treadmill
and sometimes when you think you're stuck
you're right where the universe wants you to be
waiting on it to guide you

TV Failed Me

Outside of the obvious oversimplification
Of several scenarios
Stunt men and quick-witted punch lines
Things I know to not be true
I was fooled
Families working through issues with open and honest
Communication
People taking the time to really try and understand
Or make an effort to get to know
Blended families where exes get along and not just
For the sake of the kids
Moms coming home from jail and husbands waiting
Faithfully for years
Mothers having their sons' backs
Kids staying on the right track
Friendships brewing in the workplace
Work and family gathering
Very little clubbing
Jealousy expressed through regression
Etc
TV has truly failed me
I know those were scenes over an hour or 30 minutes
Multiple takes
Edited scripts
Outtakes
Ad-libs and well-placed mistakes
But I thought fiction was based on truth
I have been failing miserably at life
Thinking people had this wherewithal and desire to
Get it right
To live this life in peace and harmony
Evolved and free
My glasses were too rosy
Or maybe it's just what I take from what I see
TV really failed me

I Know Better

I used to think I was important
I found that to be untrue
I was a tool to be used
For a brief period of time
I made you feel good
Or it felt good to be getting what you wanted
I used to think I was special
A unique refinement of life
That was a lie
I thought I mattered more than just matter
Sadly I learned I was indeed just the latter
I used to think I was someone you couldn't live without
There is no doubt that it is easier without me
At one time I was desired or so I thought
My fault
I was sure I'd never be forgotten
It was easy
I was nothing
I used to think I was hard to put down
However I was a toddler's toy
I used to think I was a cut above
Apparently that was just above the rug
A dust mite to be swept out
I once thought I was cared for
Loved and adored
Nothing more than a fable a tall tale
A fictional story
Made out of deceitful lies
I thought I was liked
I swore I couldn't be ignored
Now I'm just a ghost story
I used to think I was one of a kind
Guess not
I know better now

Windows

life situations always present you with a climactic point,
a window of opportunity if you will,
a point where hesitation can mean a difference
in the outcome,
and boldness always defines the moment.
sometimes that window has a split-second life expectancy
and can only be opened once
and sometimes it swings open several times
giving you ample opportunity to get it right.
one thing is for certain—all windows have a finite life
and should never be squandered in fear,
excuses, or doubt,
in short.
never miss your windows looking through them and not
jumping out.

What If

Maybe I am your fantasy . . .
everything you have ever dreamed of.
Or I could be your greatest transgression.
I might be the mistake you need to make to truly understand passion.
I could just be fleeting or passing–
fuck that.
Scratch that last one.
I matter.
This is life-altering shit.
Oh don't mind that, that was just my insecurity;
Arrogance.
Seriously, Miss–
I could be something you missed.
The point is this–
too often we dismiss and miss experiences we are supposed to have;
too often that guy or gal who made you nervous
was the next stage in your emotional evolution.
It's funny how all the good ones left say
there are no good ones left
but have three friends of the opposite sex
who know them best
and care genuinely.
Except–
"That's just my friend."
Seriously.
You want to know why you can never commit
or find anything legit?
Because you've been carrying on an emotional relationship with your "friends" for years!
And you have no room in your heart to let anyone else in.
It's your emotional safety net and it's keeping you blind.

Sometimes those you've been confiding in are a good fit-
think about it.
You've been pouring out the soul of you to them-
what else do you have to give?
What if that friend
was really it?

Not Their Life

All they see is the picture painted in front of them
And their entire life is built around either trying
To match or avoid the past
She wants him because he reminds her of Dad
And he won't commit because Dad's cheating made Mom sad
He watched as she cried herself to sleep
He watched as Dad packed his things to leave
Or maybe they never got to grieve
Mom died a long time ago
The pain from her death was never dealt with or let go
So there is fear
Which causes strife and pain
What's there to gain
I've often seen the playbook all too clearly
Sitting in front of her parents like this looks familiar
This is what she's after
She can see some of him in me, maybe it's the laughter
More often than not, it's the intelligence
Whatever it is
I think who they are or were to you is irrelevant
I begin to withdraw because things are
Exactly what they seem
I'm only here to fulfill your fantasy or better yet
Your dream
You're looking for someone to fit your mold
Meanwhile I want to define my path and build my own roads
I am not against tradition, but I don't like
Conditioning especially that which can't be seen
Whether you realize it or not, you'll want me to be
Just him and you'll act like she
I'm sorry both those parts are already taken
I'm looking to build my own traditions and the
Vacant part
For example, I like to spend Thanksgiving

Feeding those in need
I want my girls to decide on new themes every year
For their Christmas tree
I need someone who dares to be different
And trust me we don't always have to agree
And I swear I'm open to change
If we are defining our lives and love for ourselves
I'm sorry, I don't want what your parents had
Or didn't have
Together, let's build our own plan

I Get It

they attempt to downplay the connection's existence
because it doesn't net them the singular commitment
it all ends up in resentment
eventually finding it futile to try and finding
similar replenishment
listen
there is nothing to replace
what you're looking for is different

The End

Sometimes goodbye isn't goodbye
Sometimes never saying goodbye doesn't mean that
It's not over
But goodbye doesn't signify the end
Sometimes it appears like cold shoulders or hearsay
From a friend
I guess ours lies in silence
Or stubbornness
First to get a reply
And then refraining from trying
From imaginations running wild
To be captured in a grin

I Am

I am a Heartbreaker
Smooth with my words, charismatic, and quick on my feet
I am Discrete
I have a smile that can't be denied, a style
Undefined; I drum to a different beat
I'm Calculated, even when I appear to be moving
Hastily please savor me
For I am Refined, like a five-hundred-year-old on a
Bottle of wine
A Picasso undefaced by time
An original record with that smooth vinyl sound
I enjoy the simple things
Like sunsets, family outings, and quality time
I am Old-School
I listen to Frankie Beverly, Sam Cooke, and Etta James
I am
I am Now, Later, and then some
I am a Father and Son
One of two sets of fours always hated doing chores
I've been hit by a car twice and thrown from one too
As you can imagine, extremely thankful for life
I am not to be taken lightly
I'm not that pot you dip your finger in to see if
It's hot, there is no question about me
I am Serene but I am Mean
I never said I was a nice person
You might catch me cursing but that's not when
I am really upset
I am nothing like anything you've met so consider
Yourself lucky
Luckily I'm not arrogant, right
I love and fight, no need to stop and
Make the distinction
I love as if I've never hurt before and if you push

Me to that point
I'll beat you like you're the cause of
All my life's frustration
Like you are the reason I got punished
In the Fourth grade
I am Cool just like the other side of the pillow
I'm the Saga, as in I always continue
I am Brilliant
My two cents are more like fifty so when I repeat
Myself, you're 98 cents behind
I am geographically sound
I've been places but originally, I'm from the south
The 9th ward downtown to be exact
New-Or-leans: I embody resiliency
And yea I leave off my t-h's sometimes
On Friday you can catch me at a fish fry
I make groceries and eat red beans on Monday, and I
Can flat-out get down in a second-line
You probably don't even know what that means
And you probably never met a person like me
But don't worry, who I truly am is yet to be seen
Who I am today will soon become obsolete
I am Forever Young
I am The One
Consistency consistently
Please believe that I am who I am, I am not who was,
But I will Always be me

Life

Life like love is selfish—
as you're running along trying to keep up with it
it sometimes doesn't even acknowledge you.
And it's mean about it too,
speeding up the pace as you catch up but never
slowing down for you to ever beat it.
And should you stumble, trip, or fall, life just keeps
running along
as if you were never there at all,
no matter what you do, how well you run, or how many
times you fall.
Should you ever stop running,
and you inevitably will,
one thing is for certain through it all—
life is not concerned, and it will go on. . . .
Pace yourself, slow down, and enjoy.

Fear

I'm jumping out the window with this one . . .
but not before I put on my parachute.
Shiiiid, this ain't the first time I tried this jump.
I fell face-first last time. . . .
I mean . . .
imma jump but I ain't gon be stupid about it.
I mean . . .
I love you . . .
but . . .
what if we don't fly? What if I get hurt?
No, seriously . . . what if I get hurt?

[pause]

See the reality of love and relationships is that
you never can be too sure,
and no matter how many times you check and make
references and inferences about your mate, there is a
level of risk and faith involved.
See, you've resolved that love is a risk
and you've resolved that you and this person might
just be a good mix,
and you've EVEN resolved that this person isn't perfect,

but . . .

you've also resolved that all you want is bliss.
And though you've resolved that this ain't gon' be easy
you've also resolved that you ain't gon' put up with
this shit for the rest of your life.
You want every kiss to be as sweet as the first,
every experience to defy gravity,
every sexual encounter to be . . .

. . . this isn't reality, you realize that right?

We all have bad days!
Geeeez can I make a mistake without you digging our grave,
or puttin' me in the class like everybody else?
I'm not him, her, or them . . .
but I am at the same time if you get my drift,
and the reality is this—

you are scared shitless!

You've seen your fair share of ups and downs,
so you've hidden behind your career
or your playa-like mentality
or your men ain't shit and women are stupid fallacy.
You've taken promotion after promotion,
organizational titles to boot,
so you justify not having time for love, in truth . . .
you spend hours on end shooting the shit with your
homegirls, talkin' bout "Girl, look at him,
I mean, he cute, but he prolly ain't shit. . . .
He prolly just like the rest of these dudes."
Fellas like, "Yeah I fucked her, but she ain't worth
my time.
I mean you know, we could kick it
but you know she ain't no dime . . . and I need a
ten in my life."
Knowing damn well you ain't a seen a TEN of anything—
not a girl, nor car, not even a ten of clubs.

DECLARATION: WE ARE ALL FLAWED

But
we're all supposed to be striving to be better.

[pause]

. . . meditate on that for a sec.
Oh, so you can make a mistake and I can't?

You want me to forgive you over and over again . . .
but when it comes to me
you mad talkin' bout it's something you thought
shouldn't be.
Please, you ain't no better than me,
talking about "I ain't ready love," no nigga . . . say we!
We ain't ready or maybe we're not meant to be . . .
ever thought about that?
YOU'RE SUPPOSED TO BE WITH SOMEONE WHO challenges
YOU TO BE BETTER and makes you want to grow without
saying a word.
YOU'RE SUPPOSED TO SPEND ALL YOUR TIME PLEASING THEM.
Stop worrying about where this is gon' go.
Float; jump–
but this time leave your parachute at home.
Tell me, are afraid of being hurt or being alone?
You're right . . . stupid question–it's both.
Don't you know every experience has a lesson all on
its own?
But you're so afraid of taking a real risk.
I mean you date,
but it's only in your comfort zone.

AS LONG AS YOU LET FEAR RULE IN YOUR LOVE REALM
you will be alone!

Don't Overdo It

I guess it's a natural inclination for us all to try and protect ourselves.
I too am guilty of creating protective measures for myself at times,
either in the form of excuses, blaming other people,
or waiting on others instead of taking the lead.
There are plenty of ways to do it.
For some people, it is an unwillingness
to change a routine
adopting a mindset that doesn't allow you to feel certain emotions
(or so you convince yourself).
You tell yourself things like "Love is for suckers,"
"I am better off alone," etc.
There are all sorts of ways for people
to protect themselves.
In most cases our means to protect ourselves work.
We are afraid of getting turned down for a promotion,
so we don't apply,
or we are afraid of getting our hearts broken so we don't even try.
Sometimes protective measures are needed.
After all, we all have limits of the human kind,
and we have to take a minute to restore ourselves in all aspects of life.
For those moments we need to close and lock our doors
just for a second to catch our breath.
Don't spend too much time in your closet,
you might miss your bus or opportunity.
Our protective measures sometimes get out of hand.
There is such a thing as overprotecting ourselves.
We deadbolt the windows and doors of our existence
in order to keep bad people out;
we wear sweaters in the summertime to protect

ourselves from mosquitoes,
cover our plants in plastic,
and isolate ourselves from family and friends;
we try our best to exist in silos in all sorts of ways.
While protection is sometimes a needed measure in life,
avoid protective measures, mindsets, fears, and routines
that hinder your growth.
Sometimes we prevent good people from getting in;
we prevent good things from happening to us or for us;
we prevent or miss out on opportunities to grow,
learn, experience, change, and be better.

Selflessness Is Done in Silence

When you give of yourself,
really give of yourself, remarkable things
begin to happen.
You release into the world energy so strong it
radiates off you into the lives of those around you.
You begin to shine with a light brighter than
anything the world has ever seen—
other people can feel it.
You motivate them,
you encourage and empower them.
You empower them in ways they never knew imaginable
because your energy is so genuine.

This Body of Water

I am standing on the shore of this massive body of water
and I'm not sure of its origin but it has the
demeanor of eternity.
See it spans much further than my eyes can see.
And from what my eyes can see
it has . . .
no end.
But it's calm.
Not even impressed with the wind.
As I looked out in the wind
upon this massive body of water that has no end
I see something that I long for every day from within,
within my daily struggles.
It's peaceful and serene.
Melancholy.

So, as I struggle from within to find my
purpose and strength,
my means before my end, my portion–
just a piece . . . just a piece of mind.
And when I gather my piece of mind,
I can give you a piece of mine.
But forgive me if I try to keep the bigger
half for myself.
I'm not selfish, I just have trouble sharing this.

I sit quietly
and listen to the loud silence of this massive
body of water.
It is slow to speak and I am eager to listen.
It is slow to speak but I'm sitting here wishing
that it would just utter a word.
But still, I get nothing. . . .

It's silent out.
There is no clutter of the day,
no goodbye, salutations, or hey.
No "Baby, are you ok?"
Nobody asking me, "Where are those plans?"
Nobody asking me, "What's the plan or
what's going on tonight?"
Not even the familiar words from my mother, saying
"Baby…it's gon' be alright."
Not a peep
not even an undertone.
It is completely noiseless,
deaf, silent, soundless, and unvoiced–
the perfect place to be.

I have found stillness in the composure of this
massive body of water.
I haven't said anything to it and it hasn't
uttered a word to me
but together we have achieved a connection
unparalleled.
Synchronization of man and nature
which offers me . . . a piece of mind.

Floor It

Have you ever been on a highway road trip as a
passenger and drifted off to sleep?
I view that experience as an exercise in trust.
Think about it–
it indirectly says I trust your ability to navigate
the road so much
that I will unconsciously ride with you.
I will dream peacefully trusting you not to drive
recklessly or drastically do something that will
change our lives forever.
The motion of the car and the drive become your calm.
The only thing that wakes you is going slow–
a pitstop for gas, changing lanes to pass, or slowing
down for traffic.
It feels like as the car slows,
you become jarred from your peaceful state.
Imagine–
your peaceful dream gets disturbed.
Now you're groggy and confused.
Tired.
And what's your first question?
Where are we?
Where are we?
That's a question that floats through my mind.
I believe we are suspended in a dream
state on a lover's drive.
My eyes are closed and my heart is open wide;
I've given you the keys to my life.
All I ask is that you never slow down.
Don't wake me from my peaceful dreams.
I don't want to be jarred from my sleep–
I never want you to leave.
I am curled up peacefully like a newborn
on their mother's chest,

like I pulled 10 all-nighters for my hardest test.
Rest is what your love provides me
and "I love you" will never be enough.
But while you have the keys to my heart, keep the
pedal to the floor and don't let up.
Spare me the rest stops, traffic, and distracted drivers–
keep it above 90.
Our love provides everything we need:
fuel, food, refuge, and energy;
there is nothing or no one in between us–
not another soul on our highway.
Remove the doors and seat belts,
for my heart feels at home and at rest,
full of serenity.
I've given you the keys,
I just need you to maintain the speed. . . .

Let's All Do It

I get the premise.
All lives should be valued and there should be
consequences for those who devalue a life
or decide they have the authority to take it.
And so, from that perspective, I understand the anger
and frustration.
I just wonder what would happen if we all personally
changed our actions.

No matter where it stems from there is a lot of
negative energy being spread daily.
Sadly, negativity and ignorance get
glorified at every turn.
Maybe if we didn't promote negativity, the youth
wouldn't emulate it.
We anger at the complete disregard for our lives and
I understand why,
yet we all have family members we disown over nonsense,
coworkers we hate,
neighbors we ignore,
exes we wish ill on,
friends we betray or cut off over mere differences in
opinion and ways of living,
and people we take for granted.
All until they are gone.
In death, we speak so very highly of all that have
fallen no matter the cause.
In death, we seek to defend and avenge wholeheartedly.
I wonder what would happen if we remembered all of
the good in a person,
showed them appreciation and fought vigorously to
protect them while they were alive.
But that would be boring, I guess.
There would be nothing noteworthy to share if all we

did was uplift each other, right?
I mean who wants to live in a society where all we do is love one another? Bananas, huh?

This is the time to unite,
stand in solidarity,
promote positivity,
and show value for the lives of our people.
Evoking change is not only after a tragedy has happened.
The time for these actions is every day.
I have lived long enough to see negativity
manifest negativity,
I have also seen the opposite be true.
Spread positive energy and I guarantee it will come back to you.

Part IV

It Didn’t Work

We promised
Forever
To talk
To address things when they got rough
We swore
We’d never run
We shared
Very intimate details
Fears
Disappointments
Years
We lied

Selfish

I have spent my realities trapped in the dreams of others
Trying to make them come true
I have spent my realities doing what's best for you,
Her, and everyone else
And I think it's about time to take my dreams
Off the shelf

No Measure

Though I love you fiercely, I never quite measured up
I wasn't tall enough; big enough
Very pedestrian where you were concerned
No stamina
I loved you more than you'll ever love me
Never deceptive or egotistical
Just expansive
I wasn't trying to and I didn't know how to handle you
I was sweet; a nice guy it seems
Mashed potatoes basically; I'd never be coffee

To My Unborn

"See, I got demons in my past, so I got daughters on the way.
If the prophecy's correct, then the child shall have to pay

for the sins of her father, so I barter my tomorrow against my yesterdays and hope that she'll be . . . okay."
It's taking me some time but I realize now that I've had fun at somebody else's expense. . . .
Yours; the player now has a little girl.
See they call it a player's curse but it's more like his worst nightmare.
As he stares into her eyes, all he can think about is how to keep them dry.
Maybe I'll put a lock on her door, maybe I can convince her to only have sex after she gets married at age 44.
Maybe she won't like boys or girls and she'll just become a nun.
Maybe she won't get caught in the deceptions and lies and she'll just be cool and have fun.
But they have cried too much and far too many times-
they have felt abandoned;
they have felt alone;
they have been hurt to the point of scorn.
They all but hate you! Upset with themselves because they couldn't escape you.
It was like running in quicksand
and if he hadn't had so many stolen moments and late nights, he might not be in this fight,
this fight to keep this little girl from the hurts she'll experience in her love life-
so, what will be her vice?

Will it be the chocolate dude, different in his approach to life,
set apart from all others and vibes to his tune?
If so, she's doomed much like all those he pursued,
his seed being pursued.
This is like those steroid injections to the face.
The pain I wouldn't wish on my worst enemy, memories
I wish I could erase.
Faith is not a word that's usually associated with the game
though it often has the last say so. . . .
All I can do now is sit and watch, from the sideline of your life.
Now I know what my coach was talking bout. . . .
I feel like I'm helpless–
does it really take all this to settle the score?
She doesn't deserve it. . . .
Why does she have to deal with my remorse?
Why her?
I'm the guilty one, I'm your culprit.
Apparently, I felt like she was worth it.
Now she'll have battles to fight large and small.
They'll be times when this life will get hard

but sweetie don't get to wrap up in it.

It's not all your fault. . . .

I too am to blame for some of your bad days, your heartache, pain, and strain.

Crowded Room

As I fall on deaf ears,
in a crowded room of my close peers,
I believe my motivations aren't clear.
It's like I'm here for the same reason–
she can't be that nice,
but everything I'm saying can't be falling
on deaf ears all night.
What does she believe?
And I know her reservations are bigger than me,
but the room is still crowded, so
I think I may leave.

I Really Wanted To

I really wanted to call
But honestly
I didn't see the point
Trust me, I know the sex would've been on point
And I remember what you do to make my soldier point
And I know what it means when your chest begins to point
And I know exactly what to do to make your toes
Curl
Have you on the phone like "Guurrrl . . . let me tell you"
And so it goes

I really wanted to commit
Seriously, in the beginning, you had me smitten
I would've written down all the words to every love
Letter, a-la *Sex in the City*
I wanted you to be my Carrie and I your B-I-G
And you'd give me one more chance
But you know what they say
All doesn't end well in war and romance, but it's fair
I swear, I really wanted to dance
The music sounded great
But the reality is, you'll never get that good vinyl
Sound from iTunes, cd's, or cassette tapes
And I'm lil' bit more old school than you could take
So, we take it back to Jennifer Aniston days—*Friends*
Now you know I'm not really good at making amends
And neither one of us is high on that John Legend
shit again
So
Oh well

I really wanted to answer
I mean you attempted several mediums of communication
And after that last email

I swear I started seeing smoke signals and pigeons
Clearly, you were serious
Clearly, I wasn't tryna listen
You never listened so I figured I'd try something different
And let my silence be my medium
No translations
This monologue comes without closed caption
Or that SAP feature
And picture, that bitch ain't got no receiver either
Just an incomplete pass

I really wanted to go back
But some stories just aren't meant to have sequels
And just because trilogies are made
Them shits really only work for people like The Beatles and John Wayne
So excuse me if I don't go 'head and make your day
This shit ain't for play, this is real life
I really wanted to oblige you but mulligans are for amateurs
And last I checked, they canceled Apollo night
So I bid you goodnight

I really wanted you to feel me
But it's just something about our connections that's unyielding
Maybe I'm not giving you enough energy
Or we're not meant to be
But I'll keep on writing because you need me
You'll see . . . you'll see

The Next Guy

Dear next guy,
You're welcome
The dirty work has been done
And if you are wondering and I know you aren't
It wasn't fun
There I was on my typical journey
Looking for love
And there she was
Broken and battered lying half dead on the sidewalk
She was severely scared
Partially the last guy's fault but mostly hers
I picked her up
Shit, I don't know why
She looked like she needed a hand
I didn't realize I was preparing her for you
She couldn't seem to recall who she was
So, I reminded her
Gave her a warm bath
And very comfortable place to lay her head
My chest
She fast asleep
Per my usual, I can't rest
She confessed or proclaimed gratitude and
Fealty all the same
I laughed because at the time
She didn't even know my real name
Still calling me Mr. or the acronym ASH
I made a splash
Open doors caves and wonders she didn't even know existed
Touched buttons on her that did more than tickle
Her appeal rekindled, she felt sexy again
For you sir, she'll understand sensuality
And don't let her lie to you
She is now nastier than you think she is

Sincerest apologies for the permanent marker
And tattoos on the wall of art
I gave her the space to clean up, evolve, resolve
And I forced her to grow
Oh now, stop it, no need to thank me
If I didn't address you with this you'd never know
If I'm being totally honest
I didn't do this for you
She didn't see the love I was giving her
Until I was torn in two
Gave her all the blueprints and warning signs
Told her exactly what to do
Typically, my handwriting is bad
But I know the instructions were legible this time
Or so I thought
I am a vessel through which love flows
But never gets stuck
Anyway, you're welcome again—fuck!

Finally Done

I have no regrets about what I did
But it's affecting me
Knees weak
Separation anxiety
Seriously
We can't be
And as much as it hurts
I am worth more
Actual support from my girl
Me and the little ones are all that's left
How do I handle this lump in my chest
Several days coming without rest
Wondering what's on the other side
I'm afraid
But hoping for the best
Truly standing alone
You really shouldn't have gone
Just stay home
It's all I asked
Now there's no turning back

Pieces

Several parts
But nothing whole
Never alone
But no one to hold
Just pieces

Maybe I Never Loved Her

Maybe I never loved her;
maybe I was infatuated with her beauty,
mesmerized by her lips, lost in her eyes,
only in search of what was in between her legs—
a fantasy I never got to erase; I didn't get to check it off or out,
something still etched in my brain.
I've often wondered what it tasted like.
I think I might have to move it from my wish list to my bucket—
nah, I really loved her.
And I knew it the first time our lips touched and I remembered it the last time I saw her;
there was a rush of emotion dams could never hold and levees would surely break.
It was the cool thing to do then—
our hands were locked in place and in places I'm sure you don't know or wanna know about.
She took me places that no child my age should have gone, on any school bus route.
Like a typical teenager, I felt like I had it all figured out—
maybe not.

Maybe I never loved her,
her buttercream complexion and the supple silhouette of her curves; the way her companions sit in her upper torso and the lower portion, well—you get the idea.
She felt as real as she looked and she looked like a goddess.
Possibly the Sun God's daughter, responsible for peace and harmony.
She was amazing but I thought she was far out of my

league, so I never even bothered,
then one day I called and she answered—we danced through conversations;
she put smiles on my face;
I laughed so hard I found new wrinkles or maybe I created them.
I uncovered a delicate creature with a bit of mystery.
One I could never love because of her curse or her desire to be
and my curse was that I wanted us to be we forever—
never in a million years was she interested in me.

Maybe I never loved her.
Hell, I can remember a time when I never even liked her
but it's amazing what a summer away can do.
I used to think she was funny—
funny smelling and looking—
and then I never looked at her the same.
She still remains a fixture in my eyes.
Her eyes are a beautiful exotic color.
And I couldn't have possibly loved her;
I was apparently doing other things with other people in exotic places.
Seriously,
I love her—I loved her for no other reason than her just being.
Sure, she's arrogant and mean, but shit so I am,
so I am. . . .
Hard to find someone that down and it's not like she didn't have options;
I've seen all my competitors—I was always physically lesser;
they were all taller and bigger, both light and dark,
probably more attractive but they all fell short.
She was devoted and tied—loyalty.
Of course, I loved her and I always knew she also loved me.

Must Be Love

Queasy
Unsettled
Something's not quite right
Separation anxiety–possibly
Maybe? Definitely! Definitely my problem
Rejected the outward cry I'd been looking for
It was the right thing to do, spitefully so
There's an air of unfinished business
Or greedy cake finishing
Cause who wants to have something they can't eat
Learning how to leave well
And worse enough alone
Learning to deal with the anxiety and scars
Learning how to love the ugly way
Letting go of the temporary
Focusing less on the euphoria
And what people consider the glory of that
Ever-popular sensation
No–at this point, I am more focused on what we hate
To do when we love
Figuring out how I can be better
From the things I did wrong
Loving and losing
Opposing the alternative of choosing not to
Never regretting letting myself try
But remember it's all part of a plan
No matter what you think of the time

A Lesson

I was never right for you
I gave in too much
Meaning I gave you too much of my heart
Too much control
You needed me to be bold
Not vulnerable
You needed me to take control and mold thee
But I wanted you to be free
The persona fucked with my mind
I thought you had it all figured out
I didn't think you needed much interjection
I was drawn to what I thought was your strength
You needed my direction
A lesson

Bitter Sorrows

I believe it was the lady in red who said
You can keep your sorrys
I tend to have those lined up for me too
I'm sorry I assumed or I wasn't there for you
And I know I'm not the partner I'm supposed to be
But I'm sorry
I said I was going to be there for you
Except I had to . . . well—I am sorry
You really can keep your sorrys
I am exhausted
How about you not
How about you refrain
I know nobody's perfect
But everyone is capable of being considerate
Thinking things that matter to them through
I am not one of them and it's tried and true
So I won't be sorry
In fact, fuck you!

For the Record

I never needed you
I wanted you
I chose you
Need evokes the concept of settling
Or codependency
That's not me
I had options and still do
And if you wanted to
I'd still choose you
I want you
Unconditionally but untraditionally
Without necessity
For the record

I'm Not Mad at You

I'm not mad at you
but I'd be willing to bet a dollar or two
that you'll never understand why I chose to handle things the way I do
or did, as according to the internet we're not friends anymore
I.E.
even in my make-believe life, you couldn't continue to accept me
and believe you me, I'm sure you feel like I did you wrong
and I'm not mad at you for leaving me alone or being upset that I never returned your calls
guess you'd never believe I wasn't in my right mind
and you'd never believe that
"I just needed time, to do what I have to do, caught in the life"
well not exactly, actually I was caught in tragedy and despair
I know sweetheart, I know you care and you wanted to be there
but there was nothing you could do to save me or not much you could do but embrace me
and it's hard to do that from all the way out there
and I'm not mad, but I'm sure glad you had enough pride to leave me alone
I'm sure glad you felt like you couldn't take it anymore because you just didn't know how to help
glad I had already figured that through the thickness you wouldn't be there
you had trouble deciding whether you were gonna be there when you could be here
so how could I ever trust that you were ready to stare down that barrel with me

ready to jump off the cliff and be free, like eagles soaring high
truth is you really pulled back cause you were scared of heights
in the words of my brother Q7, "YIKES"
and church folks' favorites phrases "Jesus Christ"
when in tough times is it ever ok to retreat when it gets hard
and I'm not mad but
when is it ever ok for you to miss two free throws when you're down by one
and there is no time left on the clock
can we at least get the tie
good luck explaining that kind of choke to your coach
but all jokes and metaphors aside
I'm not mad at you, but according to the internet, it seems as if your season is up in my life
and I
"woulda came back for you, I just needed time"

Refraction

You're not the first girl I ever tried to love but
Didn't love me back
No she wasn't you
But I'm use to that
Sadly
I'm use to that
I called her radiance
But she never believed me
I spent my hard-earned on her
She ain't tell me I could keep it
And dollars never made sense to me
My money skills are poor at best
The point
I'm pouring into souls who deserve less
And that's not a shot at you or her
Not even what I mean
She
Like you
Deserved less of me
Eventually we find ourselves in the same space
Eventually all gum no matter how strong loses its taste
And it becomes hard to deal with
Your rejection isn't hard to fathom
I'll live
Believe me, this is not from a place of bitterness
These situations always remind I do the impossible
I love from a place of reflection
It's a foreign concept
For a while
I'll still be there when you need me
But there will come time I have to leave here
See your rejection is a blessing
It's a reminder that I need to keep pressing
It's the universe telling me

You don't love yourself quite enough to see
But you are progressing
I recognize the lesson
The more I love myself
The closer I get to my true blessings
You're not the first girl to not love me
I even dated some of them for years
Constantly asking myself
Why loyalty was so scarce
I mean damn
What's really going on
I've been purposely taking the long way home
For years
But I'm not a stupid guy
Not blind deaf or dumb
But I enjoyed exploring the idea of love again
Thank you for never letting me in
You prevented me from going about this all wrong
Love is reflective and free
This is what happens when I pour into a cup
That doesn't truly look like me

Goodbye

So, we've played this game back and forth for some time
I think we reached the end
Probably before the end of this rhyme
I think I'll be saying goodbye
Goodbye dear
I'm holding back the tears
I'm stronger than this
And I'm pissed
That I even feel this way about you
True I haven't always been at my best
But I did at one point put you before all the rest
And you couldn't pull the trigger
Go figure
Me the victim of my own realities and dreams
So, as I float down this stream
I reflect
And I start to reject
All who want in
Nope, not this time, I won't bend
I'll never give them what I gave you
I'll never do for them the same things
True
It's not their fault, actually, it's mine

See we've played this game back and forth for some time
Others came in and out but at the end of the day,
You were mine
And I was really yours
Though it never seemed that way
I love me too much to let things stay this way
And on this day
I sigh
And as I close this rhyme
The only thing for me to do now is to say goodbye

The Awakening

Every time they leave, I bleed
Sometimes a little or not at all
But most times it's to the point of no return
Where all is lost
Hope
Energy
Left exhausted and distraught

Every time they have left me, I have bled
Died a thousand deaths
Gasped for air because there was nothing left
Often I've given them my all
All the time despite what they think I've loved
And I've lost
But I had just enough strength to walk away
Just enough blood left in my veins
Just enough oxygen in my brain to say I cannot stay

And then she came. . . .

Part V

The Story Begins

She wanted to be my friend and I accepted
And that's where it begins
Us as friends
Having a conversation that lasts for hours
Yet I don't even have her number
The entrance in my life I don't remember
But I had seen her eyes before
We share songs, Frankie Beverly's "Lady of Magic" and
"While I'm Alone"
And while I'm alone sitting in my favorite
Spot in the house
She is reluctant yet willing to go this route
Intrigued I imagine with my imagination in check
I am enjoying the dance
She is strong and genuine, ridged and disciplined
And I am a dreamer
Her presence beseeching me
It's kind of alluring and so I dive in
At night her conversation holds me, hostage
"Sweetheart it's getting late we have got to stop
This; we're never going to get any sleep"
I mind not and neither does she
Large blocks of time keeping me detached
Yet singularly focused
Purpose Rhyme and Reason resurfaced
Calm and peace re-enter my life; Divine serenity
Storms of the past begin to waver and
Become distant memories
Even the most turbulent winds begin to cease
This is definitely clarity unleashed
And I am excited
But patient
Elated but waiting
Escaping but staying

Planted
As I rely on the true dictators' the universe and time
For it is up to them to determine her place in my life
And it feels right
Like a soft supple breeze in the wind
Clear opportunity with limitless destination possibilities
The story begins

Romance

All I need is five minutes of your time
A few seconds to hold your hand
And a couple of moments to allow my fingers to dance
Just to play in your hair
And I dare not take it any further
Maybe I'll kiss your lips, gently
Place my hand on the small of your back, neatly
And repeat. . . .

I Think You Are Beautiful

I think you are beautiful. . . .
Unlike anything I have ever seen or come in contact with
I wish I could spit, or write, or profess just how
Seeing you makes me feel
See beauty is defined as evoking one to think or
Ponder upon that which you are observing
My thought, I'm not deserving
Nor is any man walking the face of this Earth
You embody the lyrics of several sweet songs
Seeing you makes me wonder or rather explains why
I'm still alone
I think you are beautiful. . . .
Unlike anything I've ever seen
I have dreamed in the past about what a future with
You would be like
How we would have the most beautiful
Chocolate brown babies
The funny thing is, I didn't even really want kids
But I want a daughter like you
Not with just your physical attributes
Because your gorgeous exterior is nothing compared
To your flawless interior
I have loved you from day one, or maybe
It's been infatuation
Nevertheless, or whatever the case I'm definitely
Sprung and hung up on you
I think you are beautiful. . . .
Unlike anything I have ever seen
Your smile, your style, your boldness, and flare
The way you think, and the words you speak,
All make it clear
That you are by far the most beautiful
Thing I have ever seen
And I'm so unworthy, but I noticed

Dream Apart

I dream;
though I am not sleeping.
I am sleepwalking through what feels like a dream
because you are here
pressed against me in a bed we don't share.
I feel your stare and I feel I am deserving of it
cause I have stared and glared at you all night.
Anthony David plays-
"Good morning, you caught me staring at you again,
while you were sleeping, I promised GOD
I'd be your protection."
As the wind catches your hair and brushes my back
I wonder-
is this what heaven feels like?
You adorn my sweats
as we continue to rest in a bed that we don't share.
But oh, how I long for you to be there-
forever.

She Trusted Me

she trusted me
and I don't mean in the sense that mere mortals need to be trusted
because she knows me better than that
she has handed me her life
and I am grateful
and I as a man have no choice but to protect that which is most precious to me—her
when I say protect, I don't mean the average hustle and fuss about in the streets
because that's easy
but to protect the very essence of her
her inner fears and thoughts
her heart
to protect her from tears and erase her past fears
the honor of being the last man she will ever love
but what do I have to offer
I am but a mere mortal
so when she really needs something, I offer her my father
because no matter how high I lift her
she can't get to heaven on my back or my biceps
but when she is scared, I hold her
and I listen
though at times I find it hard to concentrate
see, my mind gets the best of me as I begin to daydream and drift
as I begin to count the freckles on her face
making sure every one of them is in the same place
as I left it the night before
I adore
and say thank you
she loves me

Intimacy

If I could
I would caress your face
Kiss you in all the right places
Let you wrap your legs around me any way you see fit
Legs
Head
Waist
Purity in energy

Character Love Affair

I need a Beth and Irish West-Allen
I need Mrs. Robinson
Confidence
I want my own Fiji water
Loyal
Where is Nakia with Okoye's love for Wakanda
Without challenge
I want Phylicia
Written in the stars by writing them together
Not forever but never. . . .

Random Memories

We went out
Had cartwheels of fun
Five, four, three, two, one
I released my love
Nothing more satisfying than watching your sexy ass
Body lean back
And slide
Oh My God
I could see then I had lost you
Your only focus to prove your point
Pridefully wanting to prove to me you were worthy of
Being the one
Carnal
The look
Tell me my shit ain't bomb
I confess
The shit is amazing
But it's not the only thing taking me there
The adornment of your body alone leaves me paralyzed
The sight
Your smell
In and around your nose
Doesn't get more natural than that
I can tell when you're sick or getting there
Your hair
Under the braids
Heroin
I can tell when it's dirty
Unfortunately, I am not all that familiar
With your gentle touch
But boy my sight and smell surely know of my love
Mesmerized by your eyes and presentation
Observing your preparation
I can see your mannerisms of softness

Your wheels when they're turning
The concern
The scare expectations
The little girl inside always questioning her worthiness
Hard-shell candy
Pineapples cherries and everything sweet
I do remember a time I caught you slippin
"What are you doing to me?"
That night you took off your armor
And I put it down on you
My love, ever-present verbally
Can only properly be communicated physically
So I made the most of my opportunity
Giving you all of my soul
Wonder if you noticed everything was ok
That when you dropped your guard
The world didn't come crumbling down
No criticism skepticism or disappointment in sight
No failure
Nothing but light
You were soft
Finally, you gave up the keys to the car
And I was perfectly able to drive us home
Too bad it was only a few short blocks
Maybe next time you'll let me drive
And it won't be just for the night

Love Vessel

I've been used, but not on purpose
I've been taken advantage of
As I should be
Most times
Remain unchanged
But I sometimes still feel empty
I am a vessel through which love flows
Freely I might add
I give out my vulnerability like dollars in a strip club
I give effortlessly of myself like I have
More than enough
Which is funny because my heart gets bigger every time
I grow more patient
Understanding
And refined

My Dreams

This morning I dreamed I laid my head on your chest
With my torso in between your legs
We were naked
I found rest; I felt safe
You caressed my head as we lay there
My naked skin pressed against yours
I felt every piece of your vulnerability replenishing me
I could vividly see your areolas and perfect curvature
I imagine that before I poured myself deep inside you
And left all the broken parts of my soul
This morning I dreamed I wrapped my arms around you
I was on top with a hand full of your derriere
I slowly pushed myself deep inside of you
We moved in slow motion, lava flowing
We were floating
This morning I dreamed you were in my bed
Your thick thighs spread far and wide
You put your arms around my head
As I played in between your legs with my tongue
Your moans faint but your body full of sound
You quivered
Releasing all of your frustration to me
I devoured
This morning I dreamed you woke me up
You gripped my loins and gave me your tongue
I laid my cum slowly on your taste buds
You drank my love
This morning I fantasized
You stood stout in front of me with your curvature
And definition
My hands started up your waist
To your hips
To those mountains that sit impeccably or so it seems
I've never seen 'em

I kissed in between your neck and chest, down the
Middle of your breast, to your navel
I drank from you, on my knees, hands cupped to my face
Over the banks of the Nile in a drought
This morning I dreamed that you were here
But reality woke me up. . . .

Friend of Mine

I always wondered who
and then I realized it was you.
In the words of Anita,
"It's been you all the time"-
on the school bus before Sci High,
life in rewind,
thinking about all the what-ifs and why,
But what is and what's supposed to be can't be denied,
yet I
and you concur,
that it isn't just for the birds,
that we belong to one song
holding on to one word-
love.

Grace

"I will follow you anywhere,"—this is what she said to me
Incomprehensible at first but heavy at all turns
But I know that she means it
Meant it rather
I try to gather myself to receive
I have never seen Class personified so perfectly
Never understood what true grace would look like up
Close and personally
And now
It lives in me
If I were a betting man, I'd honestly just break even
I'd bet it all that she would never have joined me
And now
I'll bet it all that she will never leave
Stories begin and end
Leaves fall from trees
Cycles begin
Again
We'll watch them come and go
Maybe one day we'll sit and watch the flowers grow
Kids will get old
Depart
And maybe return
Singing groups may break up
Ages will continue to go up
There will be plenty of ups and downs
And I don't know what it all means
But
If she's going to follow me
Then we'll see it all together
Longevity is our destiny—definitely
"Absolutely"

Invitation

I want to taste the place made for creating human beings
and create space between your knees
to insert my hip joints
as I pull you toward me
slowly
steadily
and with meaning

Reflective Irony

I am an assassin
Like the one John Mayer spoke about
And she is my counterpart
Or so I figured out
And I think that was the thing that attracted me most
And also
One of the things that tore us apart
Then ironically
Reassured us at the same time

We Are Missing It

You loved me almost effortlessly
A knack for attention
Some of it was forced
Meaning you did it to prove a point
So, you can love me naturally
Wonder if that's a specialty
Like, have you loved them all that way
Easy and effortlessly
I'm not easy to love
I mean outside of the lack of exclusivity
My point
This can't be a tactic
Something you employ at every stage
And I adore every nook and cranny of you
All the follicles
So, if love comes this easy
What are we doing?

The Leo

Sex appeal is lost on her but she is deathly attractive
Distracting at times as she walks around the room or house
She excites—no additives needed
The desire is absolutely genuine
She gives you that ride-or-die feeling
Something like a right hand or main man
That's my lil homie, definitely not homely
You could show her off
She's fine as fuck
Legs well defined, proportions in the behind
And the chest sits up
Fun size
She isn't but I want her to be mine
Until the end of time
Something to call my own, like an ace in the hole
Now admittedly she can be cold, too proud, too bold
And on my journey, she wouldn't be alone, so eventually
She'll need to say, so long
Raw, unrefined, talent physically and mentally, even spiritually
A little ways away from the trilogy
But there is something about her that keeps me interested

Intimate Daydreams

I'll start with your neck
Move to your chest
Kiss down your sides
To your thighs
And spread you wide
And stick my tongue inside
On my knees in between
Standing and feeding
She asks, "Are you full"
Never
Until it's drained
Paralyzed

Obsession in Free Verse

I watch you float across the room
wrapped in silk and milk and honey all at the same time
I am really diggin your chocolate high
why leave myself with just a hint for the night
chocolate this rich is made to be indulged in for life
will you marry me, not for tomorrow
but let's start with your yes tonight
and will go from there

Mental Quickie

I've had you on my mind
I climbed your peaks and valleys and hid
In all your alleys
And together we
Indefinitely
Transformed into pure energy
We made love
You performed well and I thoroughly enjoyed

Like You

I have never loved anyone like you, like you
At all times, I'm all ears
All in spite of
You consume my thoughts and visuals throughout the day
I take long pauses that start as five-minute breaks
The fabric of my life is stained with you
I have been fooling myself for years or maybe I've
Been operating in fear
Shit I don't know
Maybe I was afraid of how deep in love I could fall
Bottomless pits can be dreadful
This has already gotten ugly
So engulfed, I can't see you without me or me without you
However, it's supposed to go or be
I cannot be me if you are not here
Like I said "It doesn't work like that"
Unequivocally and completely, I want us to be MORE
I just want to touch you
And when I make love to you, I get in trouble
Passion erupted
Who would have thunk it
Seriously—who would've thought I'd get you
I have never ever loved anyone like you, like you

Late Mornings

Hellos and good mornings
In the form of passion
Forecast
Showers
Lightning rods to carry it
Put a ring on it
Please
I'm engraved everlasting

I Love You

I love you
I mean, I really love
Every facial expression
Gesture
I love the way you think
Well, the way you look when you think
And to think
That this would be the start of something magical
Restitution to my soul
Peace
In
Around
And through storms

When Sex Doesn't Matter

when sex doesn't matter
everyday chatter becomes erotic
conversations take you places
simple phrases set your soul on fire
words take on curvature fit for a goddess
and a sentence can have you focused or fixed
using commas to join the former with the latter
using commas like the foreplay before you begin to
exclamation points become your erections and periods
never seem to be a burden
as a matter of fact—they get you where you're going
with a period you could actually conceive
becoming impregnated with love's true seed
agape

when sex doesn't matter
your definition of what's intimate doesn't begin
with a kiss
it starts with the very mention of a name
then heightens with a glimpse of them into your visions
until this person's very "hello" sends you spinning
reminiscing
not about the last time you found your souls
intertwined in the bed
but about the sensual feeling, you got from that
kiss on the forehead
or that hand on the small of your back
you have graduated
into a realm only the mature understand
where holding a hand is like passionate
lovemaking in the sand

No Clue How We Got Here

No clue how we truly got here but I do know you saw
It before me
I initially took it as one of the deadly sins—lust
And admittedly I brushed you off
I didn't see what you saw
Then came the trust
A friendship that became a staple in our lives
We thought so much alike
We could blame that on adjacent zodiac but really,
We are just that
Similar or kindred rather
Two sides of one coin, complementary angles, the
Lyrics and rhythm of a song
We belong
We always have
No clue how we got here but I love that we got here
We love so effortlessly, it's crazy
Love in maturity
Unbounded by distance or persistence
Nothing else is needed
It's like having a great day every day and having
Everything always go right
Like giving the children the latitude to roam free
While sitting out on the park bench unconcerned
Freedom
No clue how we got here, but here we are
Confidants and counselors; a metaphoric hug and held hand
Support through the silent presence or checking in
As needed repeat
A constant cycle of acceptance, understanding, and love
Attraction: passion steadily climbing
Elevation: metaphysical spiritual quantum, we keep
Getting better
We are forever; surefire

No contradiction; honest birds
No clue how we got here

Terrain

For my 28th I desired to place my feet over the Grand
Canyon but I upgraded to your peaks and valleys
Instead of the so-called breathtaking view
I chose to listen to the intimacy of your breathing
While exploring your valleys, peaks, and mountaintops
Thundering hearts beat with perspiring curvature
Waves of pleasure sensually designed
Impatiently waiting to patiently release
Almost before your bags hit the floor, simultaneously
Climbing inside while breaking down your walls
Reservations overtaken by lamentations but only
For a moment
Fearful touch
Exhale
I found the serenity of nature I was seeking
I found the serum for believing but still I am
Doubtful of any type of achievement
Yesterday's grieving
What exactly are we seeking?

The Rise

She is unbothered. . . .
She doesn't ask me too many questions-
she's not concerned about who's calling or texting,
or who I am addressing.
She isn't concerned about whether or not I care;
never once has she asked me where
or why things are the way they are-
she's enjoying the ride.
And I'm sure she has her reservations but she
handles them well,
for the most part.
Smart, classy, sassy-an all-around beautiful person.
I found her, or rather I discovered
that when I think about how I love her-
I love her;
the world is a different place when you have found love.

www.ingramcontent.com/pod-product-compliance
Lightning Source LLC
LaVergne TN
LVHW021155160826
845679LV00024B/2129

* 9 7 9 8 9 9 5 1 1 4 4 0 6 *